The Truth about the Superior Lie:

RESURRECTING THE LIVES OF AFRICAN-AMERICANS CRUCIFIED BY THE LIE!

REVISED EDITION

Linda Seatts-Ogletree

Contents

Acknowledgments

I would like to first thank God, who is the head of my life. I give thanks to my late parents, Lowell Massey Sr., and Lillian Massey, who shared great wisdom with their children. I thank Dr. Gloria Sellers for taking the time to assist me in bringing structure to this book. I want to thank all my spiritual mentors who taught me how to be an authentic minister of the Gospel. To my son, Anthony K. Seatts II, who gave me the opportunity to accomplish the will of God and to my husband, Richard, who supports me, treats me like a queen, and loves me unconditionally. Finally, to our forefathers, mothers and all the freedom-fighters who paved the way for our present and future.

Introduction

There's a saying, "If you don't know where you came from, how can you know where you are going?" Do you know where you are going; and if you don't—why?

The Truth about the Superior Lie isn't an "academic book." However, it speaks directly to you, clearly and truthfully, about the United States of America and institutional racism. This book exposes the grip of white supremacy, and how African-Americans can break the grip, shake off, "it's the white man's fault," mentality, and bring out our inner greatness.

We reveal the truth about the "lie" the "Superior Lie" that one race of people is better than another. Too many African-Americans (I am African-American) have bought into the lie, which led to crucified lives of self-hatred, hatred of each other, and low self-esteem. We are descendants of royalty, warriors, inventors, mathematicians, astronomers, entrepreneurs, and spiritually strong people.

A Black African man was the first man to devise and execute an architectural plan to reach heaven after the great flood in the days of Noah—thousands of years before the birth of Christ.

In the beginning, God created the heavens and the earth. (Genesis 1:1)

God existed from the very beginning because He is the beginning. He created the heavens, the earth, and all mankind. After creating the world, God said, *"Let us make man in our image, in our likeness, and let them rule over the fish of the sea and the birds of the air, over the livestock, over all the earth, and over all the creatures that move along the ground"* **(Genesis 1:26–27)**. *"God formed the man from the dust of the ground and breathed into his nostrils the breath of life, and the man became a living being"* **(Genesis 2:7).** It was the breath of God that gave us life; a life that only He can give.

It is safe to say that God is the only Superior being who is over all, above all, through all—He is all!

When we go back to the Garden of Eden where mankind began, there was a river watering the garden that flowed from Eden into four headwaters. The names of the four rivers are Pishon, Gihon, Tigris, and Euphrates.

> It has been revealed plentifully in scripture geographically and physiognomically that the Garden of Eden was in Africa somewhere near, or possibly in Ethiopia. (i)

> It is suggested in Genesis 2:7–14, following the creation of the first man, the Pishon River which compasses "Havilah" was in Africa. It attained its name from a Black man named Havilah, who was the second son of Ethiopia.

Genesis 10:6–7 is affiliated to Adam's environment. Also, the Gihon River, which compass-
eth "Ethiopia: (same as Cush) from the Garden
of Eden, is mentioned as being part of Adam's
vicinity." (ii)

The Black/African race came from the descendants of Ham,
the son of Noah. The first-born son of Ham was named
Cush, (Cush means "Black"). Cush is the father of the African
peoples, and the father of the first warrior in the Bible named
Nimrod who orchestrated the building of the tower of Babel
(Genesis 10:8). Did you ever hear someone say, "Come here
you little Nimrod?" Well, they were referencing Nimrod, a
Black/African warrior, in the book of Genesis in the Holy Bible.

Many Bible scholars, theologians, and preachers are
aware of our rich heritage but purposely do not teach it nor
preach about it, which is another way of oppressing us by
preaching the curse rather than the truth. Yes, Ham, the son
of Noah, did not cover his father when he saw him lying naked. Some believe just like God covered Adam and Eve when
they were naked in the garden, Ham should have covered
his dad. Because he didn't cover his dad, Noah was angered
and cursed Ham's son, Canaan." Ham wasn't cursed; his son
Canaan was cursed (Genesis 9).

Cush wasn't cursed; it was Canaan who was cursed. It
has been said that the reason Blacks/Africans were "dark
skinned" and enslaved was because they were cursed and
that is furthest from the truth. Noah's curse wasn't directed

toward any race; the curse was directed at the Canaanite nation; a nation God knew would become wicked (read the Book of Joshua).

Don't buy into the lie! Our slavery further proves the fact that we came from a long line of survivors and warriors such as Nimrod! We come from such a strong heritage so what happened to our lineage of strength, determination, and will to survive?

Haters! White supremacists didn't want to share their power, so they used every method to oppress us. Rather than sharing the platform, white supremacists wanted to own the platform and everybody on the platform who were not white and male! We, on the other hand, wanted freedom and equality, but white supremacists wanted control and power. The strategy of the white supremacists was to destroy the "royal Black/African family" through slavery and genocide of millions of our ancestors. They stole our patents, inventions, and tried to destroy our mind, body, and soul. But rather than destroying our ancestors, they, in fact, made our ancestors more determined to overcome the Superior Lie!

The Beginning

My people are destroyed for lack of knowledge.

(Hosea 4:6)

One of the four rivers that flowed through the Garden of Eden was the Gihon River, which is believed to be the "Nile River" in Africa. Although we don't have a precise date when Moses wrote the book of Genesis, he was able to tie one of the four rivers that flowed through the Garden to Africa (Genesis 2:10–14).

> Biblical Ethiopia as used in most references was also located on the continent of Africa but was situated south of the territory of Egypt in north Sudan. The African and Cushite presence was found in various places in the ancient world including such places as Arabia, Elam-Persia, Mesopotamia, Greece, India, Phoenicia, Crete, and Canaan, not to mention Egypt and of course "Ethiopia" (Cush) in Africa. (1)

When Adam and Eve were created, they were placed in the Garden of Eden, which was also called "paradise" where

1

everything was perfect and pure. God talked with Adam and Eve in the garden. Most are familiar with the story of the Garden of Eden and the Fall of Man when the serpent, the devil, tempted Adam, and Eve to eat of the forbidden tree of the knowledge of good and evil (Genesis 3). It was Adam and Eve's disobedience that ushered "sin" and "evil" into the world; thus, pride and disobedience to God were the first of many sins.

God clearly told Adam and Eve not to eat from the tree of the knowledge of good and evil, "for when you eat of it you will surely die" (Genesis 2:17). Although Adam and Eve sinned, God called out to them, covered their naked bodies with coats of animal skin, and showed them "mercy" (which is undeserved compassion).

The love of God prevailed, and at that moment, He covered them, which was a foreshadowing of what was to come through Jesus Christ. A sacrifice was made, blood was shed, and God covered them. This was a foreshadowing of what Jesus Christ would do for all of us—be a substitute for our sins by paying the penalty of sin for all of us through His death, burial (penalty), and resurrection (He conquered death). Because of what Jesus Christ did for us, we too would have the opportunity not only to be "covered" but totally cleansed from our past, present, and future sins by the blood of Jesus Christ once we accept Jesus Christ as our Lord and Savior.

As time progressed, Adam and Eve had many sons and daughters. Cain, one of Adam and Eve's sons, turned away from God and murdered his brother Abel.

Another son of Adam and Eve was named Seth, and it was from the descendants of Seth that Noah was born. Noah was a righteous man who was blameless among the people of his time, and he walked with God. Noah had three sons: Shem, Ham, and Japheth (Genesis 6:9–10).

In the time of Noah, humanity became wicked and forgot about God, holiness, and righteousness. God became angry. God is perfect, and His standard of holiness is beyond our human comprehension. Because of God's standard of holiness, He became very disappointed in the sins and immorality of man. He decided to wipe mankind from the earth because He grieved that He created man. God breathed life into man. Therefore, His DNA is in all of us. There's a special place for God in our lives.

During the time of Noah, the earth was corrupt and filled with violence, and it was necessary for God to cleanse the land by destroying evil through the flood. The land had to be cleansed—another foreshadowing of what Jesus would accomplish on the cross—in that He would cleanse us from our sins through the blood He shed for us. Since Noah found favor with God, and God told Noah that He was going to put an end to all people, He commanded Noah to build an ark because it was going to rain for forty days and forty nights. Because Noah was a righteous man, God said he would establish His covenant (promise) with Noah.

Throughout the Holy Scriptures, God makes covenants (promises) with his people. It is reassuring to know God's covenant is established with those who have accepted Jesus

Christ as Lord and Savior. God's covenant (promise) is a blessed assurance that He doesn't break his promises.

Because of God's covenant with Noah, He commanded Noah to enter the ark with his sons, his wife, and his son's wives along with two of all living creatures—a male and a female.

God gave people 120 years to change their sinful ways, but people didn't change only Noah's family remained obedient (Genesis 6, NIV). That's just like us today. Somebody tries to advise us to make wise decisions that are beneficial to our well-being, but we don't want to listen. We wait until a flood of hell breaks loose in our lives when we could have saved a lot of the drama had we listened to wise counsel. But thanks be to God who is always there with a dose of grace (God's unconditional love) and mercy (undeserved compassion). God picked us up out of our mess when we should have stayed there because of our poor choices. Thank God for mercy!

After the waters flooded the earth for 150 days, God said to Noah, "Come out of the ark, you and your wife and your sons and their wives. Bring out every kind of living creature that is with you." The sons that came out of the ark were Shem, Ham, and Japheth.

After this second chance at life, it was necessary for Noah's family to repopulate the earth. The origin of all nations came from Noah and his family.

One day, Noah was out in the vineyard where he drank some wine and became drunk. He lay uncovered inside his tent. Ham saw his father's nakedness and told his two brothers, Shem and Japheth, who were outside. Immediately, Shem and Japheth took a garment and laid it across their shoulders. They then walked in backward and covered their father's nakedness. Some scholars believe that Ham disrespected his father and should have done what God did when He covered Adam and Eve when they were naked in the Garden of Eden.

When Noah awoke and became aware of what his youngest son, Ham, did, he said, *"Cursed be Canaan the lowest of slaves will he be to his brothers"* (Genesis 10:25). Let me stop here because there has been a lot of misinformation on who was cursed. It wasn't Ham who was cursed; it was his son Canaan. Why Canaan? There are several different interpretations of why Noah cursed Canaan. One interpretation is that God foreknew that the Canaanites were not going to make right decisions and knew they were going to behave worse than their father did. Therefore, God told Noah to curse Canaan as a nation, not a race. God can see the past, present, and future in one glance, and knows the decisions we will make.

There are so many people with the wrong interpretation that Ham was cursed. As you can read for yourself in the Bible (Genesis 9:27), Ham wasn't cursed; his son Canaan was cursed (Genesis 9). Cush wasn't cursed; it was Canaan who was cursed. The promised land of "milk and honey" was the land that God promised the Israelites. They were to drive out the Canaanites, so they could possess the land (Joshua 1–9). The Phoenicians, the Hittites, the Jebusites, the Amorites, the Girgashites, the Hivites, and others were descendants of Canaan—the son of Ham!

Unfortunately, there are many today—scholars, theologians, and just ordinary folk—who believe that the curse on Canaan is the reason Blacks/Africans were enslaved, which is yet another lie. The curse that was on Canaan was fulfilled as the Canaanites have pretty much disappeared; however, Blacks/Africans and African-Americans are still here. Furthermore, the Bible never associated the curse of Canaan with race. Of course, long before slavery, white supremacists took this scripture and "added" meaning to it to justify slavery and Black/African inferiority.

On the contrary, the slavery experience further proves the fact that we come from a bloodline of survivors and warriors because we overcame slavery.

Ham also had a son named Cush, and from Cush came the African people—Ethiopians, Egyptians, Libyans, and others. Egypt is in Northern Africa. Cush means "Black." For those who are familiar with the concordance (Strong's Concordance is an alphabetical index of the principal words in the Bible and its meaning in the original language), look up Cush, and see what you find.

Moses' Egyptian Hebrew brother, Aaron, and his Hebrew sister, Miriam, were mad at Moses because he married a Cushite (Black/African) woman (Numbers 12:1). Further, God was so angry with Miriam's behavior toward Moses that He turned Miriam's brown skin white as snow for seven days (Numbers 12:9–10).

Cush had a son named Nimrod who was an African warrior, a mighty hunter before the Lord (Genesis 10:8). Nimrod wanted to become a great ruler of a great world empire, and he attempted to achieve his goal. Nimrod was responsible for the Tower of Babel. (Genesis 10). It was Nimrod, an African man, who attempted to bring together humanity after the flood. He was the rebel, the founder of Babel, and the hunter of the souls of men. It is suggested that Nimrod also built Nineveh—the city in which Jonah was sent to preach (Jonah 1:2).

The first seven descendants of Cush are situated in Arabia or Africa close to Arabia. The sixth Cushite descendent, Nimrod, establishes the Cushite presence in southwestern Asia, both in Babylonia ("the land of Shinar") in southern Mesopotamia, and then up to the Tigris-Euphrates rivers into Assyria, Northern Mesopotamia.

Of special interest in this treatment of Cushite descendants, whose ancient presence in the Biblical world was extensive, would be "the land of Shinar."

This phrase is a definite reference to the ancient people known as the Sumerians. The Sumerians were composed of people who were

> the indigenous population of Mesopotamia and called themselves "the Blackheads." Their origin was Cushite. Shinar is mentioned several times in the Old Testament (Genesis 14:1, 9; Joshua 7:21; Isaiah 11:11; Zechariah 5:11; Daniel 1:2). Daniel 1:1–4 shows the Relationship between "Babylon," the "land of Shinar," and the "Chaldeans. (2)

Imagine that a Black/African man was the founder of the first civilization. I never heard a sermon or teaching on Blacks/Africans in the Bible. Why? With all this biblical truth, what happened to our zeal and determination to continue our legacy? With such a rich bloodline, we should be saturated with determination, discipline, and dedication to be the best that we can be.

Although we were not taught about our rich biblical heritage, our ancestors, the freedom fighters, knew they were created for victory when they overcame slavery. It started with Cush, and throughout the generations, Blacks/Africans significantly continued through biblical history.

> Some of the other great descendants of Ham is Ramesses, Bathsheba, Solomon (the richest man in the bible) and the Ethiopian Queen of Sheba, and many others. The Bible is replete with clear statements on the origin and history of the Black or dark-skinned people

and many scholars and Bible institutions are quite aware of the genealogy of Blacks, however, over the years have not given them their proper rights, refusing to link Blacks with Japheth or Shem. But it is abundantly clear from the Bible in Genesis 9:18–19, that Noah's three sons, Japheth, (Caucasian or European), Shem (Semitic or Hebrew) and Ham (Hamitic or Blacks) are mentioned as being the fathers of all people of all nations. (3)

What Happened to Our People?

Scholar and social scientist Dr. Francis Cress Welsing in her controversial book titled the *ISIS Papers* postulates that "white supremacy domination of all nonwhite people is essential for white genetic survival." *(4)* In other words, for white supremacists to remain in power and "superior," they must oppress and literally "keep" African-Americans and other people of color oppressed.

As you read in the previous chapter, traditionally, African-Americans come from a long line of warriors and survivors. We overcame slavery because we were united, and we stuck together because we needed each other as we were a "community." Unfortunately, over four hundred years later, our roots of a community have been lost. Racism exists; therefore, we need to remain kindred and connected as a community.

During our slavery experience, we relied on each other and "kept hope alive" that we would one day be free. Our ancestors literally prayed themselves out of slavery. They knew they could never give up! Why? Because they were not just thinking about themselves, they were thinking ahead. They were thinking about their children and their grandchildren. They planned, set goals, and were not self-ish or individualistic. They thought about everybody's future not just their own! This loyalty to our community is unfortunately something that has been lost today among many of our people. Our ancestors knew that God would bring them out of slavery, and He did.

You might ask, "Why did we have to be enslaved?" Only God knows that answer, but I think I can shed some light on it too. Through struggles comes strength. It was about survival, and God created African-Americans to be survivors and victors! We triumphed over the detestable experience of slavery. We came out with nothing but our dignity, unity, and connectedness as a "community of people." We stuck together, bought land, created products, owned stores, and businesses. For example, in the late 1700s, there was an African-American man named James Forten who owned a manufacturing company in Philadelphia that made sails for ships, and he employed more than forty black and white workers. Ex-slaves purchased land, men- and women-owned farms, cleaners, hair salons, manufacturing companies, grocery stores, entertainment venues, and a countless number of inventions.

In years past, it was about community because we were all we had. We really had each other's backs! Against all odds and through hope, faith, prayer, and love, we were on our way to freedom.

In the Holy Bible, we learn from the Israelites (the people God chose to proclaim His word). In the Old Testament, we find the story of how God freed the Israelite slaves from their mean slave master, the Pharaoh, but the very freedom God gave them was the very freedom that kept them in bondage! While Moses was on Mount Sinai receiving the law and commands from God to deliver to the people, the Israelites became impatient. Moses was gone too long, and instead of using their freedom to choose to wait on the message from God, they chose to build false Gods out of gold and silver and to indulge in immoral sexual behavior (Exodus 32). Because of the Israelites continuous disobedience to God, through Jesus Christ, non-Jews, (Gentiles) you and I were grafted into God's plan and were chosen to be proclaimers of His word.

Just like the Israelites, the very freedom our ancestors died for is the very freedom we have allowed to keep us down! How can this be? How can freedom enslave us?

The primary goal of the white supremacy systems is to establish, maintain and refine world domination. Slavery was about power and control.

> Like most world tragedies, the Atlantic slave trade or the European slave trade started slowly, almost accidentally. At first, the Europeans did not visit the coast of West Africa looking for slaves; they were searching for a route to Asia for the spices and the sweets they had heard about because they needed something to supplement the dull European food of that day. In general, they needed new energy, new

land, and new resources. Plagues, famines, and internal wars had left Europe partly exhausted and partly underpopulated. In the years between the first European entry into West Africa from about 1438 to the year of Christopher Columbus' alleged discovery of America in 1492, there were no slaves of consequence taken out of Africa because there was no special work outside of Africa for slaves to do. The creation of the plantation system in the Americas and the Caribbean Islands set in motion a way of life for Europeans that they had not previously enjoyed. This way of life and the exploitation of the resources of the Americas and the Caribbean Islands, after the destruction of the nations and civilizations of the people referred to as "Indians," renewed the economic energy of Europe and gave Europeans the ability to move to the center stage of what they refer to as world progress. This was done mainly at the expense of African people who are still not thoroughly aware of their impact on every aspect of world history. Education for a new reality in the African world must train African people to understand the nature of their contribution to the different aspects of world history, past and present, and the possibilities of their future contribution. (5)

So rather than have a competition of power, white supremacists felt they needed to "save us from ourselves" and
used Christianity to conquer us and bring us to America.
Although they used Christianity to conquer us, justify slavery, and bring us to America, we embraced Christianity,
and it freed us.

Some people say that Christianity is the "white man's
religion." I am here to set the record straight. You can use
anything to trick somebody, but it doesn't mean what was
used is wrong! For example, the Ku Klux Klan claims they are
Christians, but we know that God is about love and not hate.
We don't serve a God who commands us to kill; we serve a
God who commands us to love our neighbors. We serve a
God of peace.

Further, some so-called "conservative evangelicals" claim
to be Christians, yet they support the current President Trump
who clearly does not exemplify "biblical values" according to
the word of God. His words of sexism toward women, racism toward Muslims and other people of color, not to mention blatant lies and divisiveness doesn't reflect Christianity.
But some conservative evangelical groups claim him to be
Christian. That's why we must evaluate a person or group by
their actions and not their words.

> Bishop William Barber, an African-American
> social justice advocate and President of
> Repairers of the Breach, an organiza-
> tion that seeks to build a moral agenda,

eloquently reminded us on a recent segment of MSNBC's AM Joy show that "the conservative evangelicals" have a twisted theology. We are seeing a non-Christian movement being perpetrated as a massive hoax on the American public, and it is as old as the magicians of Pharaoh, against Moses, as old as the Pharisees against Jesus, and as old as what Frederick Douglas called the slave master's religion versus the religion of Christ. It has always been a part of America's construct."

The African-American people are not the white supremacist's problem. *The white supremacist's problem is the white supremacist!*

Why do you think apartheid existed for so long in South Africa? From 1948 to 1990 only 16 percent of the total population of South Africa was white, yet the South Africans were victims of apartheid, which means separatists or "apartness." Think about this for a moment. Only 16 percent of the total population was white, which means 84 percent of the population was African, yet they were oppressed and disenfranchised.

I think about us in America beginning to enjoy the Civil Rights Act, the Voting Rights Act, EEOC, and Affirmative Action when our brothers and sisters in South Africa were suffering, longing for freedom. Neely Fuller suggests,

> In most instances, any neurotic instances, any
> neurotic drive for superiority, usually is found-
> ed upon a deep and pervading sense of inad-
> equacy and inferiority. (6)

In other words, for a group of people to hate another group of people for no apparent reason means that the haters have some deep internal issues of self-hatred, low self-esteem, and other deep-rooted insecurities that need to be confronted, released, and set free. God parted the Red Sea and freed us from slavery. Surely, He can deliver white supremacists from their internal self-hatred.

A human being is made up of body, soul, and spirit. The soul (heart) is the seat of our personality, and our spirit is what animates us and gives us life. If my spirit and soul is that of love, integrity, and compassion, then my expressions and actions will demonstrate the very core of my soul.

Some of what we are experiencing today are the effects (results) of an American "superstructure" built on a foundation of racism and oppression. Why? Is it about race, or is it about power? It's about both. It's about white supremacists who are best satisfied and happy when others are not.

It is an institutionalized belief system that communicates that one group of people is superior to others. That is the lie that some of us have accepted, and that is the lie in which you should know the truth.

Unfortunately, we continue to see this play out with Trump who is a "racist" and "white supremacist." It is unsettling to have a racist leader after being led by a Black man who is one of the greatest, most brilliant Presidents in U.S. History President Barak Obama.

Trump is trying to dismantle everything former President Obama compassionately built for the well-being of all citizens of the U.S. Trump made several racist comments, during his Presidential campaign and President. His latest comment, in the context of immigration, was spoken in a White House Meeting. Trump said, "why the U.S. should not accept immigrants from Haiti and Africa, S***hole countries," rather we should accept immigrants from places like Norway (white countries.) His statement is a typical "white supremacist" declaration. It is troubling that our current leader of the free world is a racist and white supremacist. This is another example of the Superior Lie!

I have a very diverse roster of friends and acquaintances from different cultures, ethnicities, and religions. I have white friends who are comfortable enough to talk about race. Some of my white friends talk openly to me about white privilege. It is not a secret that if you are white, you have privileges over nonwhites because of the racist foundation of America. I had one friend who very openly said she felt guilty of being white because of what that means for other nonwhites. She said white privilege is unfair, and she doesn't know what to do about it. My recommendation to her was to make a difference by standing up against racist ideologies and being vocal about inequality when she is involved in discussions with her peers. I suggested that she not only correct those around her who make racist and stereotypical comments, but also stand up, be vocal and fight for equality and justice for all

When you think about it, we were used as free labor to build a country of "white privilege."

In addition to using "skin" color as a measurement of superiority, materialism was thrown into the mix. However, skin color and materialism do not define the true essence of a human being. What is the essence of a human being? It's not the color of their skin. Is it their bank account, their address, or their cars? No. Materialism does not define a person nor makes a person superior. A person may drive a better car than you or live in a bigger house than you, but that doesn't make them a better person. Materialism is external to an individual and doesn't have an impact on the "internal core" of an individual. What makes a person is their internal core, their character, which is defined by their soul, heart, and spirit.

African-Americans do not manufacture guns nor do they own drug fields nor the ships and planes that bring them into the United States. So, who are the bad guys? Is it the sellers or the suppliers? Both. Nevertheless, who are the ones that get caught? The little guy in the neighborhood selling the poison to the non-Black guy.

I will never forget a documentary I saw years ago on one of the major networks where TV reporters tracked and saw shipment of drugs coming into US ports. I was outraged and asked myself if we know where they are dropping off this poison. How come the government isn't doing something about it?

To put it simply, it's all part of a master plan. If you wear down and beat down African-American males enough, maybe just maybe they will become desperate enough to sell drugs. This way African-Americans can do the dirty work of enslaving their own people. And for what? The short-term reward of selling this poison is driving nice cars and living in nice homes, but is that something to be proud of? Can you sleep at night? Is it a long-term way of life? No! It is a way to keep African-Americans enslaved. Why be enslaved in a free world? It doesn't make sense. If the African-American male becomes extinct by death or incarceration, then they cannot bring new African life into the world. Cut off the African-American man, and you cut off the African-American race.

> The denial of full-scale employment and advancement to Black males so that they cannot adequately support themselves, their wives, and their children. In turn, large numbers of Black male children grow up without their father's guidance. This leads to frustration, depression, and failure in school. Once this atmosphere is established, drugs are placed deliberately in the Black community. The drugs are then used to "street-treat" Black male frustration and depression. The high prices for which drugs are sold provide the Black male population with the illusion that finally, they are beginning to make some money and to share in the "American dream. (7)

Some of us bought into the Superior Lie. We started believing that we were no good, defeated, and worthless. That was all a lie—a mental ploy that worked. We stopped persevering; we stopped trying. Our African-American men who historically have been disproportionately locked out of corporate America and women who got tired of the struggle decided to medicate the pain with drugs and alcohol rather than look back and draw strength from the plight of our ancestors who died obtaining freedom for us. Instead of being inspired from our bloodline, we gave up the fight and became part of the lie.

We live in a free country, but unfortunately many of us have allowed freedom to kill us. We have fallen into the white supremacist trap—the trap of medicating a pain that we don't have to own, a pain that we don't have to endure.

The whole configuration of America was built on white supremacy and racism; it is thoroughly ingrained in our society. It doesn't take a rocket scientist or a PhD to determine and evaluate there is a big power imbalance in America. For African-Americans to rise, we must know why we are behind. Where's the work? Where are the jobs? Who is in control of hiring for jobs? Where are the African-American men in the workplace?

The jobs are there. We must shake off the chains of "it's the white man's fault," so we can move forward into a free future, and get what is rightfully ours—freedom to pursue happiness and the American Dream. We have the freedom to join the roster of former President Barack Obama and become the next African-American president of the United States!

We need to take advantage of our freedom to make the right choices! We cannot allow this life to stop us from obtaining what we can achieve.

Marcus Garvey said it like this:

Man Know Thyself

For man to know himself is for him to feel that for him there is no human master. For him Nature is his servant, and whatsoever he wills in Nature, that shall be his reward. If he wills to be a pigmy, a serf, or a slave, that shall he be. If he wills to be a real man in possession of the things common to man, then he shall be his own sovereign. When man fails to grasp his authority, he sinks to the level of the lower animals, and whatsoever the real man bids him do, even as if it were of the lower animals, that much shall he do. If he says "go." He goes. If he says "come," he comes. By this command he performs the functions of life even as by a similar command the mule, the horse, the cow perform the will of their masters. For the last four hundred years, the Negro has been in the position of being commanded even as the lower animals are controlled. Our race has been without a will; without a purpose of its own, for all this length of time.

Because of that we have developed few men who are able to understand the strenuousness of the age in which we live. Where can we find in this race of ours real men. Men of character, men of purpose, men of confidence, men of faith, men who really know themselves? I have come across so many weaklings who profess to be leaders, and in the test, I have found them but the slaves of a nobler class. They perform the will of their masters without question. To me, a man has no master but God. Man, in his authority is a sovereign lord. As for the individual man, so of the individual race. This feeling makes man so courageous, so bold, as to make it impossible for his brother to intrude upon his rights.

So, few of us can understand what it takes to make a man—the man who will never say die; the man who will never give up; the man who will never depend upon others to do for him what he ought to do for himself; the man who will not blame God, who will not blame Nature, who will not blame Fate for his condition; but the man who will go out and make conditions to suit himself. Oh, how disgusting life becomes when on every hand you hear people (who bear your image, who bear your resemblance) telling you that they cannot make it, that Fate is against them, that they cannot get a chance. If 400,000,000 Negroes can only get to know themselves, to know that in them is a sovereign power, is an authority that is absolute, then in the next twenty-four hours we would have a new race, we would have a nation, an empire—resurrected, not from the will of others to see us rise—but from our own determination to rise, irrespective of what the world thinks. (7)

We cannot afford to be individualistic; we can't afford to fall into the Western, white supremacist mentality of "it's about me and how much I can get." We are not individuals; we are a community—a unified front that must not give up and throw in the towel. Rather, share the towel, strategize about the towel, and work together in determining how we are going to make the towel work for all our people.

Some people feel they don't have anything to live for. And that's a travesty. Life is hard, but it is beautiful. What makes life beautiful is having peace. A peace that passes all human understanding and that peace comes from Jesus Christ of Nazareth. It was Jesus Christ who guided our ancestors out of slavery. It was Jesus Christ who died so that we can be free from the grip of sin and oppression. It is Jesus Christ who continues to give us the strength to be victorious.

Our ancestors had a strong foundation. They prayed together, they worshipped together, and they grieved together. The Black church was the only place where our ancestors were free. The only place where "Negroes" were treated equally. Today, the church is one of the most important forms of social organization in the African-American community.

Jesus spoke these words in St. Matthew 7:24–27, "Therefore, everyone who hears these words of mine and puts them into practice is like a wise man who built his house on the rock. The rain came down, the streams rose, and the winds blew and beat against that house; yet it did not fall because it had its foundation on the rock. But everyone who hears these words of mine and does not put them into practice is like a foolish man who built his house on sand. The rain came down, the streams rose, and the winds blew and beat against that house and it fell with a great crash."

Our ancestors built their households on hope and faith in God. They prayed together; they worshipped together. Children respected their parents and knew they were their parents, not their "friends they kick it with."

Our ancestors established solid boundaries that children could not overstep. And although trouble would come–the family would not crumble because Jesus was the rock, their hope that gave them peace during the storm. God is the Superior Being the head over all (Ephesians 4:5).

The Truth about the Superior Lie

The truth about the superior lie is "no man is superior to another man." All humans, rather white, Black, red, yellow, or brown, have the same vitals at embryo—a heart that pumps our blood; we all have a soul, spirit, mind, and the same red blood flowing through our veins. Because of our human similarities, the idea of superiority and inferiority is a lie. We all are part of humanity.

Some folk may have more money, more "things," but things don't make a person superior. Of course, we all must answer to someone, so don't misunderstand what I am saying. There's a difference between "authority" and "superiority." We all have authority figures that we submit to bosses, teachers, pastors, parents, and they are our leaders because of their position. We should respect them as our leaders; however, they are not superior because of their person or the color of their skin. It truly amazes me how much emphasis and power are placed on skin color. In fact, we all have the same color pigment in our skin called melanin. The amount of melanin we have determines the lightness or darkness of a person's skin. America is obsessed with "color."

However, God has blessed all of us with gifts and talents, and the color of our skin doesn't matter to God. In the Gospel of St. Matthew, Jesus said, "I have told you these things, so that in me you may have peace. In this world, you will have trouble, but take heart" I have overcome the world" (Matthew 16:33).

Is racism a conspiracy? Yes. Are you a victim? Yes. Do you stay a victim? *Absolutely not!* A victim mentality is a stronghold! What is a stronghold? Strongholds are deep within our minds. Inferiority is a stronghold. If you are constantly shrinking back from people because of feelings of inferiority, it's because the world, the flesh, and the devil have carved a negative groove in your mind over the years. It is like being in a box and you keep trying to get out, but someone keeps putting the top back on the box. Over time, you figure—well, next time the top is opened, I am going to jump out quickly, and I am not getting back in. That's what you should do. You should get rid of that victim mentality of "I can't" and adopt the attitude that "I can," and "I will!"

President Barack Obama ran his first-term presidential campaign on, "Yes I Can," and "He Did" become the first African-American president of the United States in 2008.

The good news is that through Jesus Christ we have the power to break the strongholds in our mind through the power of the Holy Spirit. If you are a born-again believer in Jesus Christ, you can pray under the authority of Jesus Christ for the stronghold to be destroyed, and God will honor your request. We are inferior to no mortal. As we read God's word daily, we will be filled with the knowledge of His will in all wisdom and spiritual understanding (Colossians 1:9).

Many African-Americans are walking around with this "stronghold" of "I can't" and don't want to put in the time necessary to succeed. We live in such a "microwave" society that everybody wants quick results. Nothing in life is easy or quick. It takes time, but you can do it. It may take ten years or twenty years to achieve your dreams, but at least you are on your way to freedom.

One of the many scriptures that got me through many trials and tests is Philippians 4:13, "I can do all things through Christ who strengthens me." You see Jesus Christ is our liberator, our vindicator. He died so that we may live and have life more abundantly (John 10:10). The scripture says, "I can do all things through Christ who strengthens me." This means that although I might be going through life's troubles, I will make it because Jesus Christ will give me the strength to make it." This means Christ will give you strength in the dark valleys and on the sunny mountaintops.

If I would have listened to man or stopped chasing my dreams for every door that was shut in my face, I would probably be drugged out on the streets. Giving up wasn't in me. I kept thinking about the millions of brothers and sisters who died for my freedom, which helped me remember that I need to keep on going with integrity, boldness, and love.

I am here to let you know that you can do it too. I have seen too many of our people waste their lives medicating internal pain. Crack, alcohol, weed, opioids (painkillers), and nicotine are killing us. The essential point is that after the alcohol and drugs wear off, the reality of life remains. It's not about medicating the problem; it's about fixing the problem.

How did I get up from under alcohol and nicotine addiction? I was set free through much prayer and recommitting myself to Christ and most importantly establishing a relationship with God. Although I didn't see a professional therapist, it was much prayer and the words of wisdom spoken to me from my family, friends, and ministers that I was able to overcome. Let me suggest to you that some of the issues we face requires professional help and there's something absolutely right about seeking help. There is this stigma in our community that "we don't need to see a therapist or other professionals. I declare right now that at the end of the day, it's about living a healthy and whole life and if seeking professional help is the solution—go for it! I remember before me and my husband at the time, left Detroit, Michigan in 1979 to move to Los Angeles, I went on many job interviews. I could type one hundred WPM, and I remember getting hired at an accounting firm in Southfield, Michigan. However, the white young lady who hired me said that she wasn't sure I would get hired, and said the only reason she had that doubt was because I was Black. Although it has been well over thirty years since this happened, we are still faced with the same kind of racist mentality. But I am here to tell you that "you can do all things through Christ who strengthens you." With Jesus Christ on your side, nothing is impossible" (Luke 1:37).

We cannot and will not allow the superior lie to destroy us!

Anatomy of Superiority

Through power, position, and ownership, the white supremacist led you and me to believe they were "better people," because they had power, position, and ownership. But that is furthest from the truth. It is the substance of your character, your spirit, and soul that makes you the person that you are.

You may have heard people say, "The eyes are the windows to your soul." In the Holy Scriptures, Jesus spoke and said to the religious leaders, "for out of the overflow of the heart the mouth speaks. The good man brings good things out of the good stored up in him, and the evil man brings evil things out of the evil stored up in him" (Matt. 12:13).

What makes a good person is what's inside. What's in our heart. In other words, what you are inside is who you are. That is what makes you a person. A fool can drive a Mercedes just as well as a good-hearted person. A fool can drive a Ford just as well as a good-hearted person. A good-hearted person can drive a Cadillac just as a fool could drive a Cadillac. The Mercedes, the Ford, or the Cadillac doesn't make a person superior nor does it make a person inferior. The bling-bling and your address does not make you a superior person. It's the substance of a person. Your core self, honesty, compassion, and integrity are some of the attributes that make you a person of substance. We cannot allow material things to measure who we are as people.

I have never accepted the labels white supremacists have created to define who I am. Neither should you. I am not a minority, I am not inferior, and I am certainly not a second-class citizen! The same applies to you. First, you should love God and then love yourself. When you believe you are somebody, then you will be somebody.

Many people are in denial about their self-hatred. I know so many physically beautiful people who don't like themselves and are so envious of others. I believe that when they look in the mirror, they see negative images that subconsciously paint an ugly image in their minds. It's like suffering from "mental anorexia." Who you really are, and what you perceive yourself to be are two different things. A person suffering from physical anorexia can be one hundred pounds, but when they look in the mirror, they see a two-hundred-pound person. It's all in the mind.

Growing up listening to mainstream (white) media; reading mainstream magazines, watching mainstream television shows didn't give an African-American or other people of color a positive image of ourselves. What you listen to, what you read, and what you watch on TV, videos, and movies feed your mind and your spirit. It's like your mind is a computer hard drive, and the media is the data that saves on your hard drive. If all you put in your mind is negative data, then you will be become negative. But if you put in positive data, positive music, positive videos, and positive books, then your thoughts will be positive.

For example, this world is so immoral and negative that you must have some antivirus software in your mind, so you don't crash. My antivirus software is the Holy Spirit. Since I am a believer in Jesus Christ, I constantly fill my spirit and my flesh (mind) with Gospel music, hearing the preached word, reading the Word of God, and prayer. This keeps my mind from crashing. Trust me, if I didn't have the power of the Holy Spirit and the Word of God, I don't know where I would be, but I know it would not be good. The Holy Spirit is like a filter that cleans out the "debris" of the world, and He directs your thoughts and decisions. Many times, the Holy Spirit speaks to us, but we don't listen and end up making wrong decisions.

We thank God for Ebony, Essence, Jet, Black Enterprise, and African-American Family magazines and the many African-American directors, writers, and producers who are dedicated to communicating positive images of African-American people from celebrities, homemakers, parents, and ordinary people. There are hundreds of thousands of African-American geniuses, educators, inventors, artists, scientists, entrepreneurs, Fortune 500 CEOs, and the list goes on. However, do you consistently read about us in mainstream magazines? It's getting better, but we still have a long way to go.

Over the years, mainstream media was on a mission to communicate superiority and power, and most of the time these images are associated with "white" people.

> Painfully aware of their grim prospects for equality in the North, Blacks were discouraged and bitter. "Why should I strive hard and acquire all the constituents of a man," a Black youth complained, "if the prevailing genius of

the land admit me not as such, or but in an inferior degree! Pardon me if I feel insignificant and weak...What are my prospects? To what shall I turn my hand? Shall I be a mechanic? No one will employ me; white boys won't work with me...Drudgery and servitude, then are my prospective portion." Here was recognition of one of the frightening realities of northern society: America was a white man's country. (9)

This was a response from a young Black man during the 1840s. A lot has happened since then; however, I still hear similar comments in the twenty-first century. Many things have changed since the 1840s of which I will mention a few: The Voting Rights Act, the Civil Rights Act, the Equal Employment Opportunity Commission (EEOC), and Affirmative Action. These laws were put in place to "level" the playing field for people of color and women. In other words, to protect African-Americans from discrimination and thus give us some leverage in society.

When I think of pioneers such as Martin Luther King, Ida B. Wells, W. E. B Dubois, Rosa Parks, Paul Robeson, Emma Till, Marcus Garvey, Harriett Tubman, and many other warriors who did not have the laws and freedom we have today, who persevered, and who didn't give up despite opposition. It grieves my heart that we have settled for crumbs when we could have steak, or Kale. Although it is evident that this country was designed with white privilege—that doesn't take away from our privilege as equal human beings with equal opportunities.

Intragroup Conflict

What makes matters worse is the fact that some non-African-American people of color believed the superior lie and thus came to America with a superior attitude of "being better and smarter than African-Americans." Unfortunately, this intragroup conflict pits people of color against people of color, and that is disastrous too. Rather than people of color coming together to build coalitions, we find ourselves competing against not only white folks, but other cultures that have been exploited by white supremacists.

To further aggravate the situation, some of our own people who have obtained success have decided that "it's every man or woman for themselves." Thus, some of us have abandoned our culture of community and have adopted the individualistic culture of western society; we can't afford to adopt this mentality either.

The saddest depiction of this are African-American Trump supporters. How can an African-American support a blatant racist and white supremacist? Maybe one day they will have a "wake-up" call and I pray they "wake-up" soon. There is an old saying that a house divided will fall. The house of the African-American community is on the brink of falling if we don't pick up our compassion and love for our hurting brothers and sisters, and become involved in creating solutions for reclaiming our communities. It's okay to live in the suburbs if you don't forget to come back to the "community" and make a difference. In fact, I am a city girl. I tried to hang in the city, but it got so tough in my neighborhood after the market crash in 2008 that it wasn't safe for me to stay. Regrettably, I had to leave for my own safety and health. My neighborhood went from quiet, diverse to drug dealers selling drugs on the side of my corner house, in which all the customers were white. There were abandoned homes, break-ins, and gunshots. One of my neighbors across the street was a Detroit Police Officer, and his house was broken into several times. It went from a clean neighborhood to me having to clean up empty food wrappers, empty pint-sized bottles of whiskey almost on a weekly basis. I just don't understand why some of us don't want to live in a clean environment.

I remember when I was growing up there were DO NOT LITTER signs all over the place and a fine of $500 if you were caught littering. Now I see parents throwing trash out of their car windows. What kind of example are we showing our kids? Is it ok to litter your city and your property? Don't we deserve better?

Democracy Is Key

Despite all America's problems and inequalities, America is still the greatest country because of one key ingredient— "our democratic freedom."

The Declaration of Independence states that men are endowed by their Creator with certain unalienable rights; among these are life, liberty, and the pursuit of happiness. The Pledge of Allegiance of the Flag ends with the words "with liberty and justice for all." Liberty means freedom. The free man can think, write, and speak his own thoughts. He is free to attend the church of his choice, to pray, and to read his holy book. He cannot be made a slave, unjustly imprisoned, or forced to do the will of another. He is entitled to a fair trial. He can protect to petition, to defend what he thinks is right. The freedom of free men is guaranteed to each citizen in the Bill of Rights. Some of these amendments to the United States Constitution include:

- Freedom of speech
- Freedom of worship
- Freedom of the press
- Trial by jury
- The right of assembly

- The right to be free from unreasonable search or seizure
- The "Second Bill of Rights" is the thirteenth amendment, "Neither slavery nor involuntary servitude shall exist within the United States."
- The fourteenth amendment, "All persons born or naturalized in the United States, and subject to the authority thereof, are citizens...
- The fifteenth amendment, "The right of citizens of the United States to vote shall not be denied because of race, color, or previous condition of servitude."

So here you have our rights as it is written. So, what have you done with your rights? We have laws to protect our rights, but we have allowed white supremacists to "punk us." Have you been "punked?" There was a popular show on MTV called Punked where celebrities were set up in a fake situation such as a confrontation, accident, and so on, and the host of the show and the event was videotaped. Then after the celebrity is overwhelmed by the situation, the host appears saying, "You Have Been Punked," which means they thought what they experienced was a real situation, but it wasn't. The same applies to the ideology and belief that whites are superior to African-Americans and all other people of color in the United States. Superiority is not real—it is orchestrated; it is not true. We must understand that we are not obligated to accept what people say if we know it's not true. When the lie is intertwined within the culture of America, it can affect your self-esteem, and you don't even know you are affected.

Have you been led to believe you could not be anything or amount to anything? Did you grow up without a support system? Well, I am here to tell you that your dreams can come true if you are disciplined, dedicated, and determined. Living in a democratic society gives you and me the right to pursue our happiness and our dreams.

One of the most powerful opportunities we have as American citizens is our vote. Many African-Americans don't believe our vote matters, but it does. It is just as critical to vote in the primary midterm elections as well as the general elections. We are witnessing how a Republican Presidency, House, and Senate can destroy our democracy. Republicans are for the rich and democrats are for all citizens. Our current president is attempting to align the United States with our adversary Russia; however, this autocratic president didn't understand that democracy has checks and balances. When he and his administration thought they could get away with unethical practices, democracy stepped in and said, "Excuse me, your actions are out of line with our democratic system, and the rule of law." Democracy is giving them a reality check. Thank goodness for Democracy,

There are many mountains in life that we must climb— mountains of racism, sexism, ageism, classism, and even though the mountains are there—we can conquer them (Romans 8:37). Jesus spoke to the saints of God, in Matthew 17.20, that "if you would have faith as small as a mustard seed which is a tiny, tiny seed, barely as big as the top of a needle, "you can tell a mountain to move and it will move" from here to there. Nothing is impossible for you." I am here to remind you that nothing is impossible. It may be hard, but it isn't impossible.

Unfortunately, as mentioned earlier, some of us has allowed freedom to enslave our minds. Rather than taking advantage of education, which is the truest form of power (knowledge is power), some would rather perpetrate by buying, buying, and buying—designer clothes, fancy cars, but no money in the bank and no car or life insurance. I could never understand "pretending" to be something we are not. I don't want to pretend to be successful; I want to be successful. I have talked to young ladies who are wearing $500 shoes but have no money. Carrying a "Prada" purse and no money in the Prada. That doesn't make any sense. We spend so much time trying to look like somebody rather than living to be somebody.

Although I was a single mother struggling to raise my son on a lean salary when I moved back to Michigan from Los Angeles, California, one thing I did was sacrifice monthly mall trips and nail salons to save in my institution's 401K. The 401K is a fund you build for the future. Because institutions and companies deduct your contribution from your paycheck, you don't miss it, and the beauty of the 401K is that the company matches your contribution. I knew I needed to sacrifice for my future because I knew I couldn't survive solely on social security. The grace of God and my 401K allowed me to retire in my fifties after twenty years at Wayne State University. If your company or institution doesn't have a 401K, it's crucial to seek trustworthy financial advisors, so you can save for your future.

Education is another strong tool to have in your tool chest. Education is power and provides us with the leverage to get us on a close level playing field. It substantially increases our chances to get an interview and a job.

Many African-American families were not informed on how to obtain an education. Student loans and Federal Pell Grants was information that passed over many African-American families. As you may know, years ago, African-Americans were not equally counseled in high school and weren't told about financial aid options as our white classmates. Student loans do not require a credit check—everybody can receive one—and it is the only way for many people to continue their education. Many people don't know you can get an education by borrowing student loans, receiving a Federal Pell Grant or scholarships. Student loans have one of the lowest interest rates in which you do not have to start repaying your loans until you complete your education, and when you go into repayment, you can spread your payments over thirty years paying as little as fifty dollars per month. If finances are an obstacle to an education, it's worth getting the student loans to gain power to be competitive in this competitive society.

I was one of the first groups of African-Americans in Detroit to be bused to an all-white school in the 1970s. Cody

High School in Detroit, Michigan, was a magnet school that specialized in business. I remember being chased to the bus stop by some of the white students who didn't want us at "their" school. It was my first experience with racism.

During my tenure at Cody, I wasn't properly counseled on options to further my education. So, after I graduated and moved to California, it took me getting sick and tired of reading classified ads for a job I knew I could do, but at the very end of the ad, it required a degree. So, I said enough is enough, and as a single parent of a seven-year-old young man, I went back to school. Again, we have all the resources right here in our backyard, and we don't take advantage of it. True, not everybody is cut out for a four-year college degree, but there are vocational schools and training available. We need to gain some skills to bridge us toward power and leverage in this white privileged world, and education is a powerful key to opening shut doors.

We should again thank our ancestors who paved the way for us, and through their blood, sweat, and tears led to laws such as the EEOC and Affirmative Action to protect us from blatant employment discrimination. Prior to the elimination of Affirmative Action, it was a policy that opened doors for African-Americans to gain employment.

Many African-Americans have sacrificed greatness for success, and there is a difference between the two. Greatness is Rosa Parks, greatness is the teacher who enjoys teaching children, and greatness is respecting ourselves, our parents, our people, and people in authority.

There were many African-Americans in the past who risked their lives to get an education. In 1962 James Meredith became the first African-American student to attend the University of Mississippi. The Governor of Mississippi was against his enrollment; however, James Meredith exercised his "rights" and attended the university. His attendance required the protection of not only federal troops but also US Marshals. This groundbreaking event led to wounded soldiers as well as two deaths. He was one of many who paved the way for us to apply to school and attend without the need of military protection. James Meredith risked his life to get an education and to prove that "you can do all things through Christ who strengthens you" (Phil 4:13).

Think about this for a moment. Today we have the freedom and the laws to protect our freedom, and yet we won't exercise our freedom because we have believed in the Superior Lie and have given up on ourselves. We cannot afford to give up! It is time to reclaim our village! It's time to shake off the cobwebs of the lie, and digest the truth. The truth is, "Nothing is impossible with God." You are more than a conqueror! What can man do to you? Lie to you, intimidate you, but man cannot destroy you. That's what we must remember. It goes back to the very beginning of time; it goes back to choices. Are you choosing to medicate your pain rather than releasing your pain to God and seeking professional help?

Eve made a choice to disobey God, and Adam stood there and watched her and didn't stand up and intervene. This one bad choice destroyed the spirit of man. The same applies to our lives. You can make a choice to believe you won't amount to anything, and you know what, you won't. But you can make a choice to start afresh today, and regardless of the negative forces that will say, "what has gotten into you; do you know that he or she is talking about going back to school; you can't afford that." That's what your friends and some family might say because they are also suffering from mental anorexia. However, for you to be restored, you will need to separate yourself from negative people who want to keep you down. One thing you must remember is that you are never alone with God. If it's just you and God that's okay because you do want someone powerful on your side; someone who can restore your mind, your soul, and your low self-esteem. God can do it if you "choose" to allow Him into your life.

Where Do I Start?

What Do We Do Now?

If someone says something that is preposterous, don't feed into it. People will always have something negative to say. There will always be haters, but remember "Do not fear what man does to you—for God is your helper" (Hebrews 13:6). With God on your side, it doesn't matter what people say. The word of God says that man is nothing but a "vapor," a "breath." Why would you allow a vapor to control you?

The person I feel sorry for is the one in denial, and white supremacists are in denial about many things. There is a psychological behavior called "projection." Projection is an assumption that others act or perceive similarly. People have the tendency to project their behavior and issues on you. For example, a person who is cheating on their spouse normally thinks that their spouse is cheating on them. People who gossip also think that people gossip about them because that's what they do, and who they are. People who project their behavior on others think that everybody is like them. Have you ever noticed that you could be an innocent bystander when someone you know will try to involve you in their mess?

The reason white supremacists believe they are superior and hate African-Americans is because they hate themselves.

You know that old cliché—misery loves company. I am a witness to the fact that unhappy people want you to be unhappy. Hurt people in turn hurt other people!

Fortunately, we have been created with an ability to make choices in a "free society," and I choose to be free of mess, stress, drama, and lies. In other words, I am not going to become the opinion that people may have of me. If white supremacists want to think they are superior, so be it. I, however, choose not to believe it because it's a lie. Thus, I move forward to get what God has for me. I also suggest that you flush this lie down the toilet. Shake it off and seek God and his righteousness, so that you can receive all the blessings that are stored up with your name on it. God is waiting for you to receive your blessings; however, you have blocked your own blessings because you have put your faith in man rather than in God who is superior to man. God is the giver of life, light, and love.

That's why it's so important to know our history. My son used to say, "Why do I need to know the past; it's boring." I told him it wasn't boring for the millions of slaves and civil rights activists that paved the way for you and me to experience freedom and equality. If you don't know where you came from, you can eventually go back there because you were not aware of the signs of the past. Knowledge is power.

What you must do from this point is set some goals. Goals are achievable. We have tens of thousands of African-Americans who set goals and achieved them, and you can too. God is no respecter of persons. The Word of God says,

"Neither Bond nor Free, Jew nor Greek, slave nor free, male nor female, we are all one in Christ Jesus" (Galatians 3:28). Jesus is the equalizer, and since He is Superior, we need to think according to the Superior One. *"For the word of God is living and active. Sharper than any double-edged sword, it penetrates even to dividing soul and spirit, joints and marrow; judges the thoughts and attitudes of the heart" (Hebrews 4:12).*

The word of God is alive; it is full of wisdom and power to keep you sane, saved, and successful. With the incisiveness of a surgeon's knife, God's Word reveals who we are, and what we are not. It penetrates the core of our moral and spiritual life. It discerns what is within us both good and evil. The demands of God's Word require decisions. We must not only listen to the Word, we must also let the Word shape our lives.

The Word of God is a monitor and repairer of our attitude. That's why we need the Superior God in our life. Because He is the anchor and the compass that keeps us focused, free, directed, and victorious.

First, you must be honest with yourself. Have you been living in a "fog" not really understanding why you were following a certain path of destruction in your life?

Have you been suffering from mental anorexia, self-hatred, and low self-esteem? Do you have a relationship with God who is the anchor that keeps you balanced? Remember a house that's built on sand will wash away. But a house built on rock will not fall. Is your spiritual life built on the Rock— Jesus Christ? Do you know that *"God did not give us a spirit*

of fear, but a spirit of power, love and of self-discipline?"
(2 Timothy 1:7).

The only one that we should fear is God because God is superior. We should not fear man because man is just—man; he isn't superman or x-men, he is a man. From the dust, we are created and to the dust, we shall leave. We came into this world with nothing, and with nothing, we will leave. God has given us a spirit of power to do all things through Christ. That's why it's so important to build your life in Jesus Christ because with Jesus Christ comes many benefits: gifts, talents, and power. No matter what a person says or does, there is a greater power within you if you accept Jesus Christ into your heart. With Jesus, you have a 24-7, 365-day connection to heaven. You become part of the Kingdom of God with a lot of power through the Holy Spirit.

It was this same spirit of power that gave Martin Luther King the strength to lead the Civil Rights Movement. Just like God used Moses to set the Israelites free, God used Martin Luther King to set us free. The same power gave Rosa Parks the strength not to fear man but to trust God by not giving up her seat on the bus. The power that I have today, and that you can have as a born-again believer in Jesus Christ is power to love our neighbors as ourselves. The same power not to hate the white supremacists but to pray for them that they may be set free from the chains of hate and bondage. God develops our character to pray for our enemies.

It's not enough just to pray; we must act. Jesus Christ was a social justice advocate. He was among the people and fought for the least of them. We must do the same and stand up for social justice and equality. We need to connect first with a gospel teaching, preaching church, but also involve ourselves with social justice organizations.

The power I have through the power of the Holy Spirit is the power to be self-disciplined. Jesus Christ died so we could live a free and powerful life. The Apostle Paul says it like this in *Ephesians 1:19–20, "and his incomparably great power for us who believe. That power is like the working of his mighty strength, which he exerted in Christ when he raised him from the dead and seated him at his right hand in the heavenly realms."* So, the same power that was used to raise Jesus from the dead, is the same power given to the born-again believers (saints) of God that believe." It's all about what you believe. Do you believe that you are free today? Do you believe that nothing is impossible for God?

Many have died for us to be free. It is disturbing that some of us take this American freedom for granted. I often say, many people should visit third world countries where running water is a luxury, electricity is something hoped for, and a house rather than a hut would be welcomed. We don't know how good we have it in the United States, and we are just throwing it away.

It's time to speak life into your life. Do you know that *"The tongue has the power of life and death, and those who love it will eat its fruit?" (Proverbs 18:21).* It's time to speak life into your life. You need to tell yourself every day that you are uniquely and wonderfully made. The world system is designed to destroy you through your mind. A person can do a great deal of good or a great deal of hurt both to others and to themselves through the tongue. Today there are many who kill themselves daily through their own tongue. On the other hand, there are many who have strengthened their own life or received comfort through the tongue. Therefore, you must guard your heart and your tongue.

It's important that you keep your mind functioning through positive affirmations. In my infant days as a Christian, one of the many things I did to stay mentally and spiritually renewed is write affirmations. Early on, I would write them on a three by five index card taped on my mirror. Today I use a notebook. Affirmations are different sayings that I speak aloud as needed. For example, some of my affirmations would say:

1. God Loves Me.
2. I am strong.
3. I am smart.
4. I will not worry about who doesn't like me.
5. I won't sweat the small stuff.
6. No weapon formed against me will prevail.

As I conclude this part of my morning devotion, I read aloud some of my strength and warfare scriptures because every day there is spiritual warfare or God is trying to grow us through trials and tribulations. When you are living for the Lord, we need to be prepared. These scriptures help me get through the day because I know when I walk out of the door, the devil will use someone or something to try to take my joy, or God will be "growing" me through a test or trial and to be victorious, I must be prepared.

Remember the antivirus software? You must run the software to get updates, and our mind needs to be updated and strengthened through the Word of God. Some of my favorite strength scriptures are **Psalms 62, Psalms 27, Psalms 37, Psalms 121, Matthew 5:3–12, 1 Corinthians 13, Isaiah 40:28–31, and 2 Tim 1:7.** Then I am ready for the day because I set the tone for the day. I do not allow the world to set the tone for me.

The last part of my morning devotion is repeating these affirmations right before I leave for work or other destinations. Was it necessary for me to repeat these affirmations? Yes. I was speaking life into my life. No matter what Superior Lie might come my way, I don't receive it. I don't even sweat it because I am walking and living under a greater power. You see we are already defined, and we should not let the oppressor define us because God has already defined and positioned us for victory!

Our minds are powerful, and we must measure our thoughts against something other than the negative messages of the World system. What better way to measure your thoughts than against the Word of God. In **2 Corinthians 10:5b, it says, "and we take captive every thought to make it obedient to Christ. And we will be ready to punish every act of disobedience, once your obedience is complete."** In other words, if our thoughts are submitted to God's control, we will remain sane and free. The Word of God teaches us how we should live and think. *"All other sins a man commits are outside his body, but he who sins sexually sins against his own body. Do you not know that our body is a temple of the Holy Spirit, who is in you, who you have received from God?" You are not your own, you were bought at a price. Therefore, honor God with your body"* *(1 Corinthians 6:18–20).*

So, in a world of The Purge and the Sons of Anarchy, you need a gauge to lead and guide your decisions.

The moral fabric of the world is woven with "Anything Goes," and an "Anything Goes "mentality will destroy you. That's why I speak my affirmations every day. I am speaking life into my life since the world speaks lies into our life.

I also strongly suggest you become part of a Bible-teaching Christian ministry. Fellowship with others helps you draw strength. Remember the church was and still is instrumental in encouraging and uplifting our community.

Remember you have rights. You have a right as any other citizen of the United States to live where you want to live, to obtain a job, education, and start your own business. Your rights might be questioned and challenged but remember our ancestors gave their lives for you and me to be free today. Don't allow freedom to kill you; let freedom build you into the person who God has bestowed you to be. Share your wisdom with others so one by one we rise, side-by-side, and step-by-step.

What I love about God is his grace and mercy; they are new beginnings. We have another opportunity to get it right.

Face your pain whether it's drugs, alcohol, sex, gambling, and so on, and contact the appropriate agency, therapist, or rehabilitation center. Perhaps you didn't graduate from High School, you have an opportunity now to complete your G.E.D. Maybe, you have been thinking about returning to school, do it! Contact a university, community college, or vocational school, and set up an appointment to see a financial aid officer, so they can discuss your options. Remember each day is a new day to make changes in our lives. Nobody can hold you back or stop you except you. Each day is a new beginning. It all begins with you. Don't ignore another day of opportunities and freedom. Remember, do the right thing. Don't let the blood, sweat, and tears of our ancestors be in vain. Most importantly, don't let the blood of Jesus Christ be in vain. Through the blood of Jesus, we have a new life, salvation, power, victory, and eternal life. If you don't take advantage of our freedom, somebody else will.

I want to share a paper my son wrote over ten years ago when he was twenty-one years old. It was for his class on the subject, "What Makes You Special." He was a senior at Michigan State University, and I was a single parent.

What Makes You Different or Special?

I have very strong beliefs and I follow my heart in every decision I make and action I take. I have a passion for helping others and improving their situations the best I can. I am a positive person and I try to stay humble. I don't possess qualities of a follower, have never been viewed as one and this is what makes me a great leader. Honestly, there are a lot of qualities that make me exceptional. Along with my honest and loyal heart comes a wonderful personality. As a physical therapist, I think it is extremely important to have a genuine and outgoing personality. It should help patients trust you and adapt to comfort easily.

What Are Your Three Best Qualities?

One of my best qualities is the amount of strength I have. I can withstand a lot of pressure and different situations without breaking down. This allows me to keep trying harder and doesn't slow me down toward my goals. It doesn't alter my attitude and thinking when in a school or work environment. A lot of this comes from my mother but most of it comes from God. He has allowed me to experience certain things only to make me stronger. Every time I go through something I look at it as a test, a test to see if I am strong enough to keep going and put whatever it is beside me. Staying strong in the worst times, having faith, and still thanking him always produce blessings in the end.

Another great quality I possess is my listening skills. I am a great listener; many people find it easy to talk to me. I don't think that I know it all and I am not afraid to hear someone out whether it is an explanation or just advice. Being a good listener can provide comfort and can also gain trust.

Another one of my best qualities happens to be dedication. I can be very loyal and dedicated to something. Since I have a compassionate heart this quality will go a long way in the field of physical therapy. This will allow patients to really see and feel that I care about their well-being and that I want to help them recover as painless and fast as possible.

Who Is the Most Influential Person in Your Life?

My mother is easily the most influential person in my life. She is an extremely strong individual. She has juggled so many burdens at once; it is kind of hard to believe that she hasn't had a nervous or severe emotional breakdown. Even if she is having a really bad day or has come across some bad information, she will still greet you with her remarkable smile that is honestly priceless. My mother has made a very positive impact on my life. She has shown me how to be a man, how to respect people, manage problems and stay strong in this very harmful world we live in today. She has helped me make it where I am today, all by herself with no father figure to assist her (now that's what I call strong). She has also shown me the true meaning of dedication. Growing up in the streets of Detroit, there were a lot of things that I could have easily got into, but her dedication to have a successful son and not lose him to the streets was remarkable. She kept me active even in serious financial times. I began to see what she was doing and thank her dearly for it. She is also a very humble person. I have never known or heard my mother brag about anything she may have come upon, accomplish, or achieved. Therefore, she is the most influential person in my life because she instilled all these qualities within me. I have become a very smart and respectable young man and I owe it all to her."

Words to live by

- "I can do all things through Christ who strengthens me." (Philippians 4:13)
- Actions speak louder than words.
- Only the strong survive.

I was so touched when my son sent me this letter. How did I do it? After seven years of marriage, my husband and I separated when Anthony was two months old. Living in Los Angeles, California, at the time, with no family was so hard. I had a dream of the white picket fence and being married forever. But it didn't work out, and here I was by myself, with a cute two-month-old baby, three thousand miles away from Detroit. Like I said earlier, God sees the past, present, and future in one glance, and He put people in my life for that season of my life. Most importantly, the first thing I did was made a covenant with God after my marriage failed. A covenant like Hannah did with her son Samuel (I Samuel 2:27–28). I asked God to raise my son and to protect him. My goal in life wasn't about me, it was about him. I vowed that I was not going to lose him to the streets. Therefore, I made sacrifices.

I remember when we lived in Los Angeles, we would take a change of clothes to church with us, and then after service, we would change in the church restroom then go straight to basketball practice. We struggled so much. Los Angeles is an expensive city to live in, and we struggled when my child support stopped coming in. I worked as an Assistant Director for Marketing at a hospital in East Los Angeles. I remember many days going to the cafeteria to charge food on my work badge, so my son would have dinner to eat.

After I returned to Detroit fifteen years later, I would take my lunch hour and leave work to pick him up to participate in youth programs. I remember working for temporary agencies until I could get a full-time position and was able to go back to school at night to get a master's degree. I would take my son to tennis practice, bring my books, and study in the car or at the facility while he practiced. I kept him so busy. I kept the legacy of thinking about my children not just myself, and it paid off.

Was it easy? No. There were many nights of crying and much prayer and financial struggle. Without Jesus Christ as my Lord and Savior and my supportive family, I could not have done it. I gave my son a spiritual foundation. Again, without a foundation, you will fall. It goes back to us living in a "microwave society." I could have made choices to make some "quick" money, but I didn't. I hung in there trusting in God for strength. From the time of my marriage broke in 1984, I struggled financially. In 1999 I began to get some relief, and after thirty years of being divorced, God sent me my soul mate in 2014. We married six months after we met, and he treats me like a queen. I could have settled, but I waited because I deserved to be with a good, financially stable Christian man. After all, I am a gift to him!

When people see me now, they may think I have always had it easy because people don't know your story, they just see the glory. But I have gone through some tests and trials that only God could get me through. Today, people want the promise without the process. If you are going to make it in this world, you must go through the process, and that's where many people decide to give up the journey.

That's why it hurts my heart now that young ladies are deciding to have babies before marriage, and that 40 percent of single parents are living in poverty. It is a struggle to live off one paycheck. If you can barely keep a man when you are married, what makes you think you can keep one if you're not? It is my prayer that our young ladies and young men will stop playing with eternal beings because that's who we are when we are born.

That's why I wrote this book. In the hopes that young men and women will begin loving and believing in themselves to be all that God has predestined them to be. A gun doesn't make a man a man. On the other hand, character, integrity, and most importantly, God makes you a man. It's time to stop letting the world dictate how you are supposed to react, look, and talk and start letting God take control of your mind, so that you can teach the world a few things. I leave these words with you, ***"May the God of Hope fill you with all joy and peace as you trust in him that you may overflow with hope through the power of the Holy Spirit." (Romans 15:12)***

Be strong and of good courage. If you want a change in your life, and you have not accepted Jesus Christ into your life, read these words aloud,"

> Lord Jesus, forgive me for all my sins. I repent from my ways. Wash me in your blood and cleanse me from all unrighteousness. I believe that you died on the cross, were buried and on the Third Day, God the Father raised you from the dead. Right now, Lord Jesus, I open the door to my heart and I receive you into my Heart, as my Lord and Savior.

If you repeated this with a sincere heart, you have been born-again in Jesus Christ. You have been sealed with the Holy Spirit (Ephesians 1:13–14). Now, you need to be baptized in water. Then you should ask God to fill you with the Holy Ghost. It's not just profession of your faith; its possession of your faith. You must seek God daily and live according to His word. You need to fellowship with a Christian bible-teaching church that teaches the "full Gospel" not just part of the Bible. You can't have a relationship with God without holiness, so you want to be part of a church that believes in holy living and spiritual gifts.

It's not enough just to pray, we must act. Jesus Christ was a social justice advocate. He was among the people and fought for the least of them. We must do the same and stand up for social justice. We need to connect first with a gospel teaching, preaching church, and involve ourselves with social justice organizations like Black Lives Matters, NAACP, National Action Network, Black Vote, Women's March, and more.

Now that you are born-again, there's important information you need to know. You can order my book, ***My New Life: A Handbook for Born-again Believers,*** " on Amazom.com or at createspace.com. This book will explain everything that has just happened in your life and what you need to do to be victorious. It's time for you to be all that God has purposed you to be. You are free!

We would love to hear your feedback. Please send us an e-mail at thesuperiorlie@gmail.com. Also visit our website at www.faithhopeministries.org. God Bless you.

Notes

(i)   Hawkes and Wooley, *Prehistory, and the Beginnings of Civilization*, 1.

(ii) Dillard William, *Biblical Ancestry Voyage*, 13

(1)   McCrary, *Black Presence in the Bible*, 103

(2)   Ibid., 8

(3)   Dillard William, *Biblical Ancestry Voyage,* 47

(4)   Welsing, *The ISIS Papers*, iv

(5)   Clark, "Education for a New Reality in the African World."

(6)   Welsing., 4

(7)   Ibid., v.

(8)   Marcus Garvey Official Website, http://www.marcusgarvey.com/.

(9)   Takaki, *Iron Cages*, 112

Bibliography

Asante, Kete Molefi. *The History of Africa*. New York: Routledge, 2007.

Clark, John Henrik. "Education for a New Reality in the African World." The Africa Within. http://www.nbufront. org/MastersMuseums/JHClarke/EdRealityAfricanWorld/ EdWorldPart9.html

Dillard William, LaRue. *Biblical Ancestry Voyage: Revealing Facts of Significant Black Characters*. New Jersey: Aaron Press, 1989.

Dubois, W. E. B. *Africa. It's Geography, People, and Products. Africa. It's Place in Modern History*. New York: Oxford University Press, 2007.

HarperCollins Atlas of the Bible. New York: HarperCollins Publishers, 2008.

Hawkes, J., and L. Wooley. *Prehistory and the Beginnings of Civilization*, 1. 1963.

Life Application Bible. New International Version. Grand Rapids: Tyndale Publishing House, Wheaton and Zondervan.

Marcus Garvey Official Website. http://www.marcusgarvey.com/.

McCrary, Rev. Walter Arthur. *Black Presence in the Bible. Volume 1, Teacher's Edition.* Chicago: Black Light Fellowship, 1990.

Takaki, Ronald. *Iron Cages: Race and Culture in 19th Century America*, 112. 1979.

Welsing, Francis C. *The ISIS Papers.* Chicago: Third World Press, 1992.

About the Author

Rev. Linda Seatts-Ogletree is the founder of Faith and Hope Ministries, International, an outreach and teaching discipleship ministry. She is the CEO and president of Release and Refresh Women's Empowerment Series, Inc., a nonprofit ministry dedicated to improving the mental, spiritual, and emotional health of women and girls. Rev. Seatts-Ogletree has walked in her ministry call for over twenty years. She served as adjunct faculty at Wayne State University (WSU) and Ashland Theological Seminary. With over twenty-five years of leadership, teaching, and counseling experience, Rev. Seatts-Ogletree is a "marketplace" minister reaching people across the globe.

Rev. Seatts-Ogletree pastored six years at Center of Hope Ministries, International, an evangelistic ministry she planted in 2001 in an underserved community in Detroit, Michigan. After overcoming stage three breast cancer in 2007, she continues to spread the word of victory and hope. She is the author of three books: *Did I Say That? How to Communicate in Everyday Life*, *The Truth about the Superior Lie: A book to Resurrect the Lives of African-Americans Crucified by the Lie!* and *My New Life: A Handbook for Born-again Believers*. You can also tune into her weekly "Seeds of Hope" radio broadcast on www.gospel440am.com.

Rev. Seatts-Ogletree holds a Bachelor of Arts degree in Business Administration/Marketing from The Union Institute in Los Angeles, CA; a master's of arts degree in Christian Ministry from Ashland Theological Seminary and a Master's of arts in Dispute Resolution from Wayne State University in Detroit, MI. She has traveled throughout Southeast Asia, Europe, and Africa where she traveled with Liberian President Ellen Sirleaf-Johnson. She is married to her soul mate, Richard, and she enjoys spending time with their children and grandchildren.